Discover and Share

SEASIDE

Angela Royston

W

About this book

The **Discover and Share** series enables young readers to read about familiar topics independently. The books are designed to build on children's existing knowledge while providing new information and vocabulary. By sharing this book, either with an adult or another child, young children can learn how to access information, build word recognition skills and develop reading confidence in an enjoyable way.

Reading tips

★ Begin by finding out what children already know about the topic. Encourage them to talk about it and take the opportunity to introduce vocabulary specific to the topic.

★ Each image is explained through two levels of text. Confident readers will be able to read the higher level text independently, while emerging readers can try reading the simpler sentences.

★ Check for understanding of any unfamiliar words and concepts. Inexperienced readers might need you to read some or all of the text to them. Encourage children to retell the information in their own words.

★ After you have explored the book together, try the quiz on page 22 to see what children can remember and to encourage further discussion.

Contents

Words in **bold** are in the glossary on page 23.

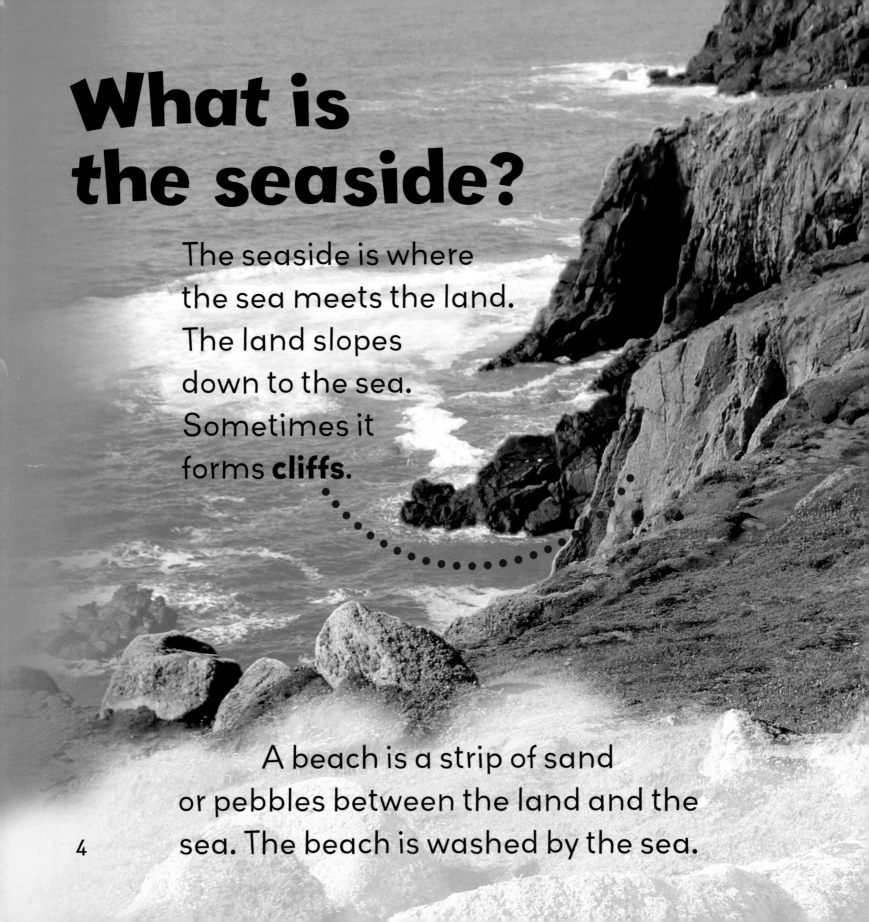

What is the seaside?

The seaside is where the sea meets the land. The land slopes down to the sea. Sometimes it forms **cliffs**.

A beach is a strip of sand or pebbles between the land and the sea. The beach is washed by the sea.

4

Here is the seaside!
This beach has lots of pebbles.

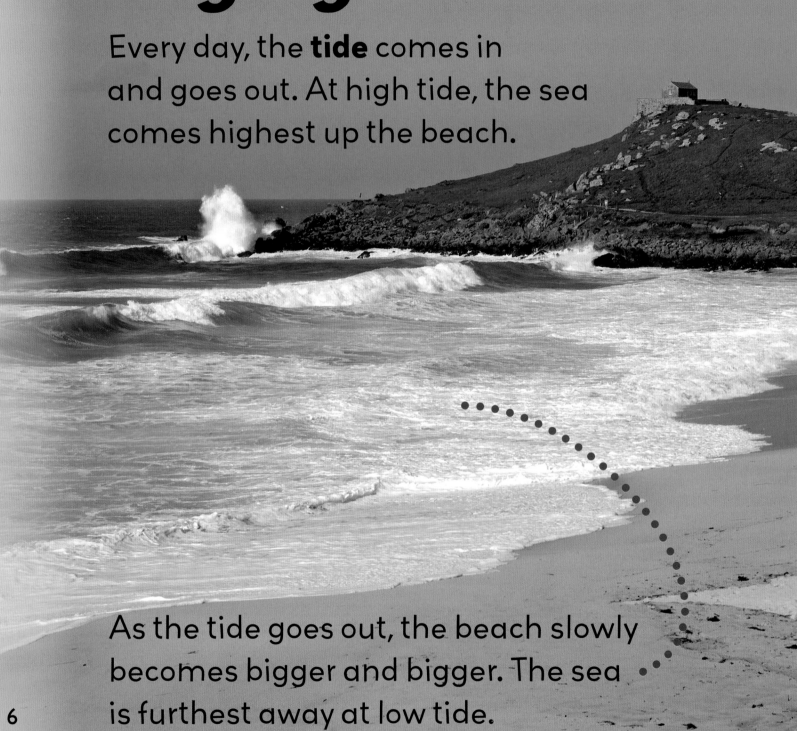

Changing tides

Every day, the **tide** comes in and goes out. At high tide, the sea comes highest up the beach.

As the tide goes out, the beach slowly becomes bigger and bigger. The sea is furthest away at low tide.

The sea splashes onto the beach. The beach gets bigger when the tide goes out.

Building sandcastles

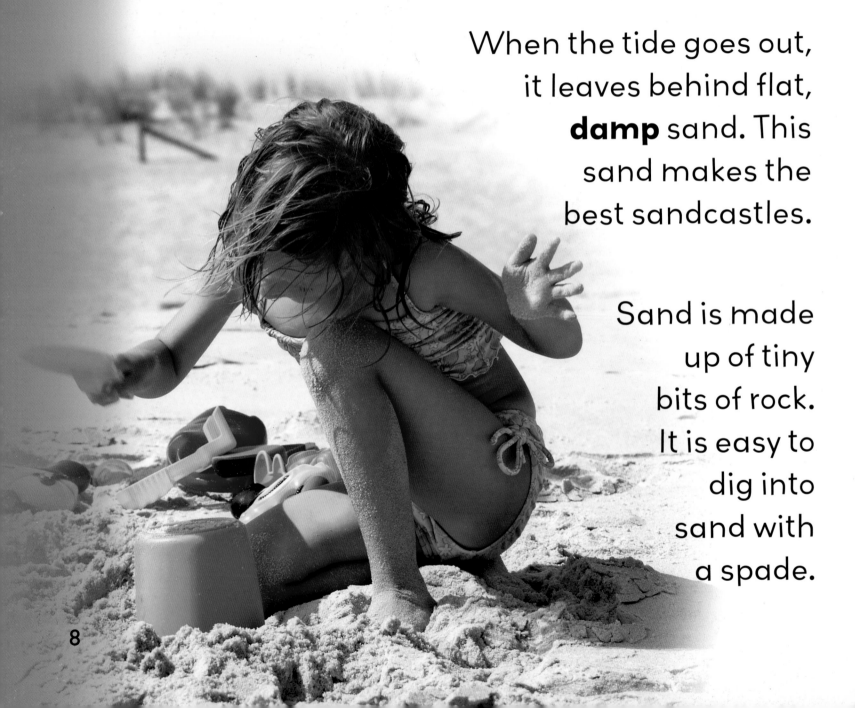

When the tide goes out, it leaves behind flat, **damp** sand. This sand makes the best sandcastles.

Sand is made up of tiny bits of rock. It is easy to dig into sand with a spade.

The sea makes the sand damp. Damp sand is good for making sandcastles!

9

Sea shells

These **shellfish** are mussels. At low tide, you can see mussels clinging to the rocks.

The hard shell protects the shellfish from **predators**, such as fish. When the shellfish dies, the sea washes the empty shell onto the beach.

This shell has a mussel in it.
The shell keeps the mussel safe.

11

Crafty crabs

Many crabs hide under stones and in the sand when the tide goes out. A crab is a kind of shellfish.

A crab has two **pincers**, which it uses to hold **prey**. They can also nip your toes or fingers!

Crabs are shellfish.
Look out for them when
the tide goes out!

Rock pool

This is a rock pool.
You can look for small
sea animals here.

14

A rock pool is a good place to see small sea animals. The pool fills with seawater when the tide comes in.

A sea anemone looks like a plant, but it is an animal. Some anemones cling to the side of a rock pool.

Going fishing

Many different kinds of fish swim in the sea. People use fishing boats to catch fish and shellfish to eat.

Some fishing boats use a fishing net. They drag the net through the sea to catch fish or shellfish.

Fish swim in the sea.
We can catch them with a net.

The harbour

Boats are left in the **harbour** when they are not being used. The harbour shelters the boats from the waves.

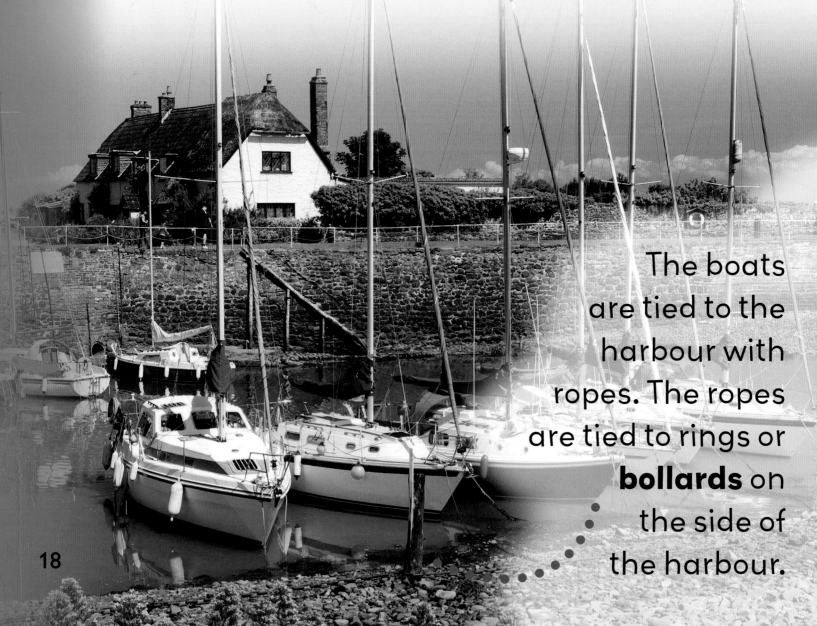

The boats are tied to the harbour with ropes. The ropes are tied to rings or **bollards** on the side of the harbour.

18

The boats are safe here. They are tied up so they cannot float away.

9

Sea breeze

There are lots of ways to have fun at the seaside. People like to swim in the sea when the water is **calm**.

When it is breezy, waves splash onto the shore. People use the wind to sail and **windsurf**.

Have fun at the seaside!

Quiz

1. What kind of sand makes the best sandcastles?

2. What kind of shellfish is this?

3. Where do some sea anemones live?

4. What is a bollard used for?

Glossary

bollards special posts for tying boats to
calm when the sea is still or has only small waves
cliffs steep land next to the sea
damp slightly wet
harbour a sheltered place where boats are tied up
pincers special claws that crabs use to grip things
predators animals that eat other animals
prey animals that are hunted by other animals
shellfish an animal with a hard shell, such as a mussel, which lives in the sea
tide change in the level of the sea
windsurf to travel across the sea on a board with a sail

Answers to quiz:
1. Damp sand.
2. A mussel.
3. In rock pools.
4. To tie boats to a harbour.

Index

This edition copyright ©
Franklin Watts 2014

Franklin Watts
338 Euston Road
London
NW1 3BH

Franklin Watts Australia
Level 17/207 Kent Street
Sydney
NSW 2000

ISBN 978 1 4451 3655 4
Library ebook ISBN 978 1 4451 2500 8

Dewey number: 508.2

A CIP catalogue record for this book is
available from the British Library.

Series Editor: Julia Bird
Series Advisor: Karina Law
Series Design: Basement68

Picture credits: Artproem/Shutterstock: 19, 22br. O. Bellini/Shutterstock: 11, 22cr, 23b. Sergio Bertini/Dreamstime: 3b, 15. Brocreative/Shutterstock: 21. Jaroslaw Grudzinski/Shutterstock: 4. Vitaly Krivosheev/Shutterstock: 3c, 9, 22cl. Tamara Kulikova/Shutterstock: 7. Kuttelvaserova/Shutterstock: 10. Marcia van der Meer/Alamy: 13. Juriah Mosin /Dreamstime: 14, 22bl. Myroslav Orshak/Shutterstock: front cover. Monty Rakusen/Cultura Creative/Alamy: 16. Stephen Rees/Shutterstock: 6. Sculpies/Shutterstock: 20. Sunshine Pics/Shutterstock: 1, 12. Tom Thulen/Alamy: 17. Nico Traut/Shutterstock: 3t, 5. 2265524729/Shutterstock: 8. Ian Woolcock/Shutterstock: 2, 18.

Printed in China

Franklin Watts is a division of
Hachette Children's Books,
an Hachette UK company.
www.hachette.co.uk